Black Beauty

Anna Sewell
Adapted by Julie Sykes

Illustrated by Natalie Ball

Contents

Chapter 1:	My first home	5
Chapter 2:	Breaking me in	10
Chapter 3:	A stormy night	15
Chapter 4:	The fire	20
Chapter 5:	Emergency!	28
Chapter 6:	'We'll never see them again'	33
Chapter 7:	The bearing-rein	39
Chapter 8:	An accident	43
Chapter 9:	Ruined	49
Chapter 10:	A London cab horse	54
Chapter 11:	The Sunday cab	60
Chapter 12:	Poor Ginger	65
Chapter 13:	'This cab is taken'	69
Chapter 14:	Changes	73
Chapter 15:	Hard times	79
Chapter 16:	Home	85

CHAPTER I

My first home

My first home was a green meadow with a pond full of rushes and water lilies. I was a small black colt* with long legs and brown eyes, and the meadow seemed very big. I kept close to my mother and fed from her milk until I was old enough to eat the grass. Then Mother went back to work and I only saw her in the evening.

I wasn't lonely. There were six other colts in the meadow and we had great fun together. Sometimes we played rough, and once, after lots of kicking, Mother called me over to her.

'Listen,' she said. 'It's time you learned some manners. Horses must not bite or kick. Your grandfather was a champion racehorse and I hope that you will grow up to be a fine horse too. Be gentle, work cheerfully and never kick or bite, even when you are playing.'

My mother was a wise old horse and I never forgot her words. Our owner was a good man too. He hated to see a horse badly treated and once he sacked a worker who threw stones at us.

When I was nearly two, something awful happened that I never forgot. It was early in the morning when I heard the cry of dogs.

'Hounds,' said the oldest colt, pricking up his ears.

'It's a hunt,'* said Mother. 'It sounds like they've found a hare.'

Soon a pack of dogs ran into the next field shouting, 'Yo! Yo-o-o! Yo! Yo-o-o!' Men wearing green coats and galloping on horses followed them. It was so exciting that I wanted to gallop too. At the bottom of the field the dogs lost the scent of the hare and ran about sniffing the ground.

Suddenly they stopped sniffing and raced back up the field towards our meadow. A stream with a high bank ran between the two fields.

'Look!' cried Mother. 'The hare.'

A frightened hare dashed past. The dogs chased her across the bank and stream, then they all thundered across our field.

As the huntsmen followed, there was an awful shriek. The dogs had caught the hare!

A huntsman held it up by its leg and everyone was pleased until they saw what was happening by the stream. Two horses had fallen, one in the stream and the other on the grass. A muddy wet rider struggled out of the water but the second rider lay still on the ground.

'He's broken his neck,' said my mother.

'Serve him right,' answered a colt.

I thought the same until Mother said gently, 'You mustn't say that. We are horses. We do not know why men take part in such a dangerous sport.'

Rob Roy, one of the horses who'd fallen, had broken his leg. Someone went for a gun and he was shot in our field. This upset my mother as she knew Rob Roy and said he was a very special horse. Years later I was very shocked to learn that Rob Roy had been my brother.

The riders all fell silent as the dead man was lifted up, then carried away. He was George Gordon, the squire's only son. A few days later, we heard the church bell tolling for George's funeral. A hearse pulled by black horses went by with lots of people following in carriages.

A dead horse and a dead man, and all for the sake of one little hare.

CHAPTER 2

Breaking me in

As I got older, I became handsome with a soft black coat, one white foot and a pretty white star on my forehead. At four years old, my owner decided it was time to break me in. My carefree days as a young colt were over. My life would be very different now.

Breaking a horse in means that he is taught to wear a saddle and bridle* so a person can ride on his back. The horse must do as the rider says, even if he is tired, hungry or not feeling well.

At first, I hated the bridle and its hard, metal bit.* It went between my teeth and over my tongue and was held in by straps that fastened around my head. It was a bad thing and I didn't want to wear it. Luckily my owner was a patient man and with his kindness I learned to put up with it.

Then, when I could carry a man, I was taught how to wear a harness* and pull a carriage. During my training I also learned to go in a double harness with my mother.

'Always do your best,' she told me. 'Even if your owner is ignorant* or cruel. And remember that I am very proud of you.'

Being broken in had come as a great shock to me, but I was lucky. I had a kind and gentle

owner and he taught me well. He even took me to see a steam train so that I wouldn't be scared by the terrible noise it made. It was something I was often thankful for in my working life. If only all horses could be treated like this.

Shortly after this I was in for another shock. I was sold to Squire* Gordon. This was the beginning of my working life and I never saw my mother again.

The squire was my owner's friend and he lived in a very large house in the village of Birtwick. I was to be called Black Beauty. The squire's wife chose my name because she said it was just right for me.

At Birtwick Park I quickly made two new friends – a sweet grey pony called Merrylegs and Ginger, a chestnut mare with a white flash on her forehead. Ginger was tall and pretty but with a bad habit of biting.

Life was very different at Birtwick Park. I was a working horse and I had to stand in a stable until I was needed. The coachman in charge of the horses was called John Manly and the stable boy's name was James. I decided I was very lucky,

for both John and James were kind and thoughtful and treated all of us horses well.

The only thing I missed terribly was my freedom. How I longed to run and play in the meadow or stand dozing in the shade of the trees. Now I was only free on a Sunday. If the weather was nice, all the horses were turned loose in the field. We had great fun rolling, galloping or standing together under the apple trees, and talking.

Ginger and I worked well together so we were often paired up to pull the carriage. During this time Ginger told me about her life. 'I didn't have a good start like you,' she said. 'I've been overworked and cruelly treated. I don't trust people and that's why I bite.'

I felt sorry for Ginger, but John was an excellent coachman and he tried hard to cure her of her habit. He and James both treated her kindly and soon Ginger stopped biting and learned to trust them.

CHAPTER 3

A stormy night

One blustery day in late autumn, John and I had to take my owner on a business trip. The weather was extremely windy, but I was pulling a light cart so I was able to go quite fast. At the toll gate,* the squire stopped to speak with the toll man before we crossed the low wooden bridge over the river.

'Don't be late back,' the man warned. 'We're in for a bad night. The river's rising fast.'

The weather quickly grew worse. We passed soggy meadows and crossed a flooded road where the water came up to my knees. At last we reached our destination, but the squire's business took ages and it was late before we could go home. The trees swayed wildly as the wind tore through them and we were pelted with twigs and leaves. I couldn't wait to get back to my nice warm stable.

Suddenly there was a terrible cracking noise. Overhead an oak tree groaned, then crashed to the ground. Its ripped-up roots landed right in front of me. It was terrifying and I wanted to run away, but I'd been taught not to so I stopped where I was, trembling with shock. John

jumped down from the cart and his calm voice soon soothed me.

'The road's blocked,' John told the squire. 'We'll have to turn round and go home over the wooden bridge.'

It was almost dark when we reached the bridge. The middle was flooded, but not too badly so the squire ordered me on. But as I stepped onto the bridge I knew something was wrong and I stopped dead.

'Go on, Beauty,' said the squire, tapping me sharply with his whip.

Still I didn't move. Something was terribly wrong and there was no way I was going any further.

John leaped down from the cart. 'Come on, Beauty,' he said gently.

I stayed where I was, wishing I could tell John how I felt.

'Get along there!' shouted the squire, from the cart.

Suddenly the door of the toll-house crashed open and a man ran out.

'STOP!' he yelled. 'STOP! The bridge is broken in the middle. Don't try to cross or you'll fall in the river.'

I'd been right not to move!

John was amazed. 'Well done, Beauty!' he cried.

It was very late when we finally got home. The squire's wife had waited up and she ran out of the house calling, 'Thank goodness you're safe. I thought you'd had an accident.'

'We nearly did, but Black Beauty saved us,'

said the squire proudly. 'He's a brave and clever horse.'

That night John gave me a special dinner and there was extra straw in my stable.

CHAPTER 4

The fire

One cold day in December, the squire came to our stable with good news for James. The squire's brother-in-law needed a new coachman. He wanted a young lad that he could train up, and James was asked if he would like the job.

'I don't want to lose you, James,' said the squire. 'But you're a good man and you deserve this chance.'

James started his training at Birtwick Park. When the squire and his wife next visited friends, James had to drive them. It was a long journey with an overnight stop, and Ginger and I pulled the carriage. James drove us well and on the first day we went thirty-two miles.

That night we stopped in a large hotel in the

market place of a town. After the squire and his wife had got out, Ginger and I pulled the carriage under an archway and into the long yard with stables and coach houses.

Two ostlers* came to help James. The head ostler took off my harness and rubbed the sweat from my coat. James waited with us until we were bedded down in a clean stable with a good corn feed.

Later in the evening, the assistant ostler brought another horse into the stables. While he was grooming it, a man came to talk to him. I didn't like the man much, and the ostler said, 'Do me a favour, Towler. Stop smoking that pipe and get me some hay from the hayloft.'

Dick Towler climbed up into the hayloft and brought down some hay. When the ostler had finished his work, the two men left the stables and I finally fell asleep.

In the middle of the night something woke me. The air was thick and choking and it stung my eyes. I could hardly breathe and I could hear Ginger coughing.

The trapdoor to the hayloft was open and something strange was happening up there. There was a soft rushing noise and lots of crackles and snaps. By now the air was thick with smoke. It was very frightening and I knew there was danger.

Suddenly the stable door burst open and an ostler ran in carrying a lantern. He untied a horse and went to lead it out of the stable, but the horse was too scared to move. The ostler tried another horse and when that horse wouldn't budge, he came to me. I wouldn't follow him either. Danger was all around me but I was too terrified to move a step.

Fresh air came rushing through the open stable door and I breathed it thankfully. But with the air, the rushing sound grew fiercer. Through the bars of my empty hay rack* I saw a red light flickering on the wall.

'FIRE!'

The cry came from outside and now flames were licking around the trapdoor. I snorted and kicked the door, and just when I was really starting to panic I heard a voice I knew.

'Steady, Beauty, easy does it.' It was James and his gentle voice was music to my ears. Calmly he patted me. Then he put on my bridle, and taking a scarf from around his neck he tied

it lightly over my eyes. 'Come on, boy,' he said softly.

I've never been so scared in my life. But I trusted James, and the scarf over my eyes stopped me from panicking because I couldn't see anything. Slowly I followed James out into the yard. He handed me to someone else, then darted back into the stable.

'James!' I whinnied as he disappeared.

James didn't turn back but my shrill cry saved Ginger's life. After the fire was over she told me that it was only hearing me outside that had given her the courage to follow James.

The yard was noisy, and people were running around shouting to make themselves heard over the top of the roaring flames. Then, from inside the stable, came an awful crash. Where were James and Ginger? Seconds later they appeared from the burning building. Poor Ginger was coughing so badly she couldn't speak.

The squire pushed his way through the crowd. 'James, my brave lad,' he said. 'Are you all right?'

James shook his head. He couldn't speak either! By now the fire was blazing through the stable roof.

'Stand back! Stand back for the fire engine.'

Two horses clattered into the yard pulling a heavy engine. Several firemen leaped to the ground and pulled out a long hose.

'Come along,' said the squire. 'Let's get these horses out of the way.'

The squire and James led Ginger and me out of the yard and into the market place. It was quiet there. Stars twinkled in the black night sky and the air was crisp and cold.

'Take the horses to that hotel over there,' said the squire, pointing to a large building. 'Order them anything you want. I have to go back to my wife now.'

The squire hurried away at the fastest walk I've ever seen.

Then a terrible shrieking started. It sounded like a horse was in dreadful pain. The noise was so awful that Ginger and I stopped dead, but there was nothing we could do to help.

The next morning the squire visited us. 'My wife is too upset to travel,' he told James. 'We will continue with our journey tomorrow.'

James was a hero, and the squire was very pleased with him. But Dick Towler, the ostler's friend, was in deep trouble. The fire had started because he'd accidentally left his pipe in the hayloft. Ginger and I had had a lucky escape. Two horses had died in that burning stable.

CHAPTER 5

Emergency!

Before James left, a new boy came to help John in the stables. Little Joe Green was only fourteen and at first Merrylegs didn't like him.

'He's too rough,' he complained. 'He doesn't know what he's doing.'

Joe was keen to learn and worked hard, and after a bit even Merrylegs agreed that he was going to be fine. But we were very sad the day James left and knew we would miss him terribly. Little did I know then how badly I would suffer without James to take care of me!

One night, not long after James had gone, I woke to the sound of running feet. Suddenly

John burst into the stable calling, 'Wake up, Beauty. It's an emergency!'

The squire's wife was very ill and John had to ride to town to fetch the doctor. In record time, John had saddled me up and we were galloping on our way. It was a frosty night and it felt good to be speeding across the silent countryside. A clock was striking three when we finally clattered into town. John rode me up to the doctor's door and banged on it as hard as he could.

At last a window opened. Doctor White, in pyjamas and a night cap, leaned out. 'What's up?' he asked.

'Mrs Gordon's very ill,' panted John. 'The squire thinks she's dying.'

'I'll be right down,' said the doctor, slamming the window.

Moments later the front door opened.

'My horse isn't fit to be ridden,' said the doctor worriedly. 'Can I borrow yours?'

'Beauty has galloped all the way here,' John answered. 'He should rest, but as it's an emergency you can take him.'

John stroked my neck while we waited for Doctor White to get ready. 'Do your best, Beauty,' he told me.

I was hot and tired but I didn't want to let John down. On the way home I galloped like the wind even though I was exhausted, and I was very glad when we reached Birtwick Park. I struggled up the drive, and as Doctor White went inside the house little Joe led me back to my stable. My legs were shaking and I was drenched in sweat.

Poor Joe! He didn't have a clue what to do with me. He rubbed me down but he didn't know that he should cover me with a warm rug to stop me from getting a chill. Then he gave me

a whole bucket of icy water. It tasted delicious and I drank it all not knowing how ill it would make me.

Soon after Joe had left me, I started to feel unwell. At first I began to tremble. I was deadly cold and my whole body ached. As the night passed, I felt worse and lay moaning in the straw. How I wished for John, but he was still walking home. It was ages before he got back, but when he did he heard me moaning and he came straight to me.

'Beauty, you poor thing,' he said, 'What's wrong?'

John covered me with warm rugs, then ran to the house for hot water to make me some gruel.*

I drank it all and at last I managed to sleep.

I was sick for several days with an inflammation* on my lungs that made breathing so painful.

John nursed me the whole time and even the squire kept visiting.

'My poor Beauty,' he said. 'You saved my wife's life but made yourself ill.'

It was good to hear that Mrs Gordon was going to live. John told the squire he had never seen a horse gallop as fast as I had the night we went for Doctor White. I think my grandfather, the racehorse, would have been proud of me.

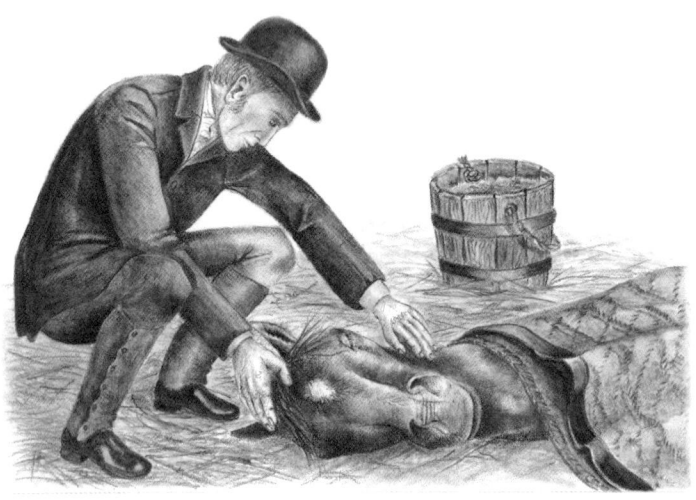

CHAPTER 6

'We'll never see them again'

John was extremely cross with Joe for making me ill. Joe worked extra hard to make up for his terrible mistake, but he was too small to do some of the jobs like riding Ginger and me. Then, one day, the squire needed to send an urgent message and only Joe was free. Here was his chance to prove himself!

'You will have to ride Black Beauty,' said the squire. 'But please be careful.'

Joe rode me very well and we passed the message on and came home. On the way back we saw two horses and a heavy cart of bricks all stuck in the mud.

'Get on!' roared the coachman, cruelly whipping the horses.

'Stop!' shouted Joe. 'Please don't hurt those horses. It's not their fault that the cart is stuck. If you take some of the bricks off it'll be easier to pull the cart free. I'll help you.'

'Get lost!' yelled the coachman angrily. 'Just mind your own business.' Then he carried on beating the horses.

Joe was furious. I'd never seen him so mad! He turned me around and rode like the wind to the brick maker's house.

'Mr Clay, come quickly,' he called. 'Your horses are stuck in the mud, and your coachman is whipping them to death.'

'Thanks, Joe.'

Mr Clay dashed out of the house to rescue his horses. Joe was so angry he rode me home at a smart trot. He didn't calm down until he reached the stables. There, he told everyone what he'd done, and John was pleased.

'Well done, Joe!' he said. 'You did the right thing.'

Several weeks later, we heard that the brick maker's coachman had been taken to court for cruelty to horses. It was the making of Joe. Overnight, he turned from a timid boy to a confident young man.

I'd been at Birtwick Park for three years and I was very happy. How could I know that change was on its way? My whole life was about to be turned upside down for the worse!

We horses knew that Mrs Gordon was often sick. But it was a huge shock when we learned that the doctor had told her she must move to a warmer country or she would die. Of course the squire wanted to go abroad at once. In no time at all, Birtwick Park was sold and all of us horses were sent to new homes.

Merrylegs was given to the vicar's children, and I was pleased for him. The vicarage would be a good home, especially as Joe had been given a job there too. John decided to give up being a coachman, and train young horses instead. He would be good at it. John had an excellent manner with us and I was going to miss him.

Too soon, the day came for the squire and Mrs Gordon to leave Birtwick Park. Ginger and I had the sad job of taking them to the station. With heavy hearts we made that journey. Everyone was very quiet, and at the station Joe buried his face in my coat to hide his tears. As the train left, John said quietly, 'We'll never see them again.'

He drove us home in silence. Only Birtwick Park was no longer our home. Ginger and I had been sold and we were off to a new life with a new owner.

38

CHAPTER 7

The bearing-rein

Ginger and I were sold to Lord W* who lived at Earlshall Park. Our new home was much bigger than Birtwick Park but it was nowhere near as nice. One of our first jobs was to take Lady W out in the carriage. Lady W was very smart and she was horrified when she first saw Ginger and me.

'Why aren't those horses wearing bearing-reins?' she shouted. 'Get their heads higher, right now. They're not fit to be seen.'

At that time it was the fashion to drive a horse in a horrible thing called a bearing-rein. The rein pulled a horse's head right up and held it there. It might have looked good but it was extremely uncomfortable for the horse and made his job much harder. How could you pull a carriage properly with your head stuck up in the air? It put strain on a horse's windpipe and ruined many a good horse.

Politely, Mr York the coachman explained to Lady W that Ginger and I were not used to wearing a bearing-rein. 'They need time to get used to it before their heads are pulled up.'

'Rubbish!' said Lady W, and she made Mr York pull our heads higher.

Those first trips out were very uncomfortable. My neck, back and legs ached badly after each outing. But worse was to come. A few days later Lady W was going to visit the duchess. She was late and in a bad mood when the carriage was taken to her.

'I'm fed up with this,' she said. 'Get those horses heads up, right now!'

Mr York shortened my bearing-rein, and although it was horribly uncomfortable I stood quietly.

Not Ginger! She remembered how badly she'd suffered in her old life before Birtwick Park, and she panicked. The terrified Ginger reared up, hitting Mr York on the nose and almost knocking over the groom.* Mr York tried to calm her but Ginger was too upset to calm down. She kicked and reared until finally she kicked her leg over the carriage pole and fell over. She caught me on my hindquarters as she went down, and I snorted with pain.

Then Mr York threw himself on Ginger's head, pinning her to the ground before she hurt anyone else. 'Untie the black horse,' he ordered. 'Quick!'

I was very angry and felt like kicking and rearing, but I remembered my training and stood still. Ginger was led away by two grooms, then Mr York came to look at me. 'Blast those stupid bearing-reins,' he muttered crossly.

My leg was swollen and painful, and Mr York ordered a groom to bathe it in hot water and treat it with ointment.*

◆◆◆

Ginger was never put in the carriage again. One of Lord W's sons took her as a riding horse. I wasn't so lucky. I still had to pull the carriage with my head tightly reined up. How I hated it! So did my new driving partner, a horse called Max.

'It will shorten our lives,' he warned me.

Four long months I suffered that bearing-rein. My mouth was always sore, my windpipe painful and it hurt to breathe. How I missed John and the squire! They had cared for me so kindly and they had also been my friends. Here I had no human friend at all. Each night, after work, I returned to my stable feeling sore, worn out and very depressed.

CHAPTER 8

An accident

Early in the spring, Lord W and some of the family went away to London. Mr York went with them. I was left at home as a riding horse. Those were happy days. Lady Anne took a liking to me. She called me 'Black Auster',* and she rode me out with her brother, Lord George, and her cousin, Blantyre. The men took turns to ride Ginger and a lively horse called Lizzie.

Lady Anne was an excellent horsewoman and one day, when taking a message to Doctor Ashley, she decided to ride Lizzie for a change. Blantyre and I went with them. When we arrived at the doctor's, Lady Anne said she would wait at the gate with us horses while Blantyre walked up the drive with the message.

'It'll be safer if you come with me,' said Blantyre.

'Why?' asked Lady Anne, laughing. 'What's going to happen to me here?'

Lizzie and I stood patiently while we waited. Soon a boy came along driving a herd of horses. He was cracking a huge whip and the horses were jostling each other. Suddenly a young colt broke away from the herd and crashed into Lizzie. Badly startled, Lizzie kicked out, then bolted with poor Lady Anne hanging on for dear life.

'Help!' I neighed. 'Help!'
I snorted and pawed the ground until Blantyre heard me and came running down the drive.

Immediately he leaped into my saddle and gave chase. It was very exciting! I sped after Lizzie and Lady Anne until the road divided and we lost them. Which way had they gone?

A woman raced out of her house. 'That way!' she shouted.

We were off again and soon I saw Lizzie in the distance. I galloped after her but the road was twisty and she kept going out of sight.

Finally we reached the common. This was a dangerous place. The ground was very uneven and it was easy for a horse to trip and fall. But Blantyre urged me on, and with his expert riding we covered the ground safely and caught up with Lizzie just before a big ditch.

Lizzie didn't stop. She cleared the ditch in one leap but stumbled on landing and fell heavily. Blantyre groaned.

'Come on, Auster,' he said, putting me at the jump.

I took the ditch with a huge leap and made it safely to the other side. But what a sad sight met me! Lady Anne had fallen from Lizzie and lay in the heather. Her face was chalk white and her eyes closed.

'Annie!' cried Blantyre, leaping from me. 'Annie, are you all right?'

Lady Anne didn't move, even when Blantyre loosened the collar of her riding habit. Wildly he looked around and seeing two men cutting turf he shouted to them. Blantyre couldn't leave Lady Anne so he asked one of the men to ride for help on me.

'Black Auster is a good, safe horse,' he said. 'He'll look after you.'

The man was not a confident rider but he quickly learned to trust me. I carried him as carefully as I could back to the doctor's house and then on to Earlshall to tell the rest of the family about the accident.

At Earlshall, a carriage was sent to bring Lady Anne home. A messenger, riding Ginger, also went to find Lord George. It was a long, anxious wait for news and I couldn't settle until Ginger came back.

'Lady Anne's fine,' Ginger said. 'She's awake.

She's too shocked to speak but she hasn't broken any bones.'

I was very glad. Lady Anne was a good person and I didn't wish her any harm.

Two days after the accident, Blantyre came to see me.

'Well done, Auster,' he said, patting me. 'You're a brave horse and your courage helped save Lady Anne's life.'

CHAPTER 9

Ruined

While Mr York was in London, a man called Reuben Smith was left in charge of the stables. He was clever and he was excellent with horses. The only trouble was he had a drink problem.

One day, Reuben rode me into town. He left me at the White Lion inn, telling the ostler to have me ready at four sharp for the ride home.

Four o'clock came and went but there was no sign of Reuben. I waited patiently and it was nine o'clock before Reuben finally came to collect me. I could tell at once that something was wrong. Instead of the polite, gentle person I knew, Reuben was loud and pushy. It was clear that he had been drinking!

'Did you know that your horse has a loose shoe?' asked the ostler politely.

'Tough! It can wait till we get home,' snapped Reuben, leading me out of the stable.

Reuben rode like a mad thing, whipping me to make me go faster even though I was galloping flat out. My shoe grew looser and more uncomfortable and I wished I could stop. Then suddenly my shoe fell off. Reuben didn't notice and forced me on over the stones. They split my poor hoof and it was so sore.

Bravely I kept galloping in spite of the terrible pain. But I couldn't keep it up and suddenly I stumbled and fell on my knees. Reuben flew to the ground. He landed heavily, groaned once and then fell silent. I felt like groaning too but I managed to struggle up. My knees were in agony and I wished that Reuben would get up and take me home. He didn't.

It wasn't until around midnight that help finally came. I was so glad to hear a voice I knew, coming from close by.

'Ginger!' I whinnied as my old friend came along pulling the dog cart.*

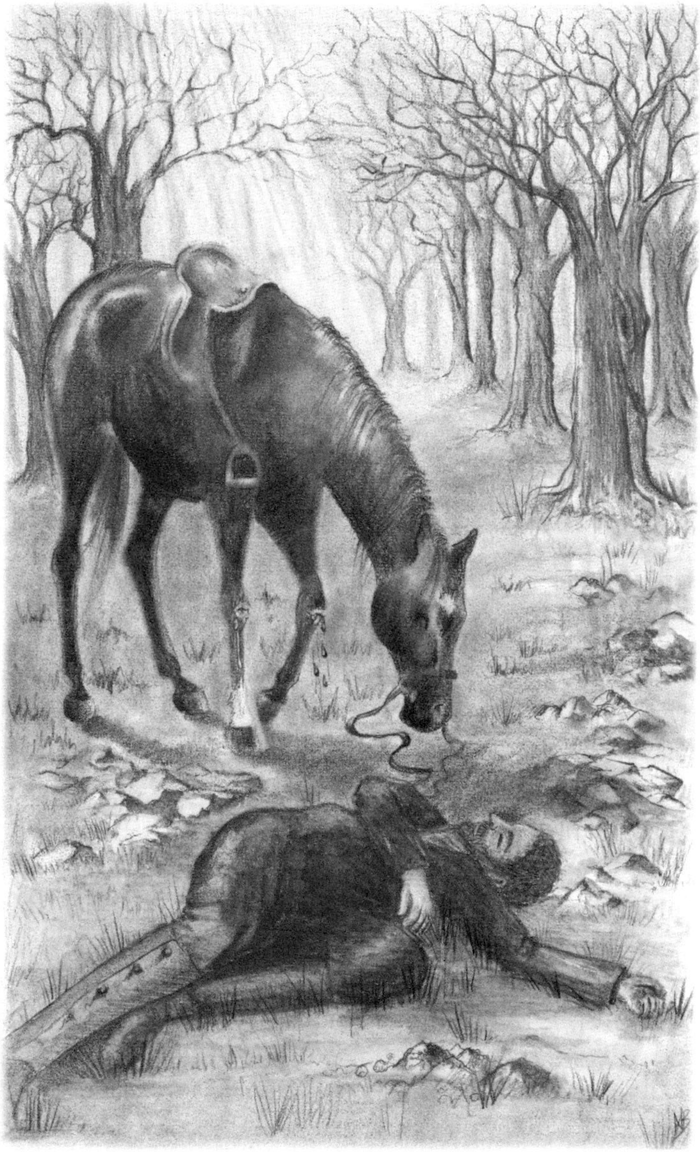

Two men were riding in the cart and they were very glad to see me.

'Thank goodness we've found them!' said one, jumping down and running over.

'Oh no!' exclaimed the other. 'Reuben's dead! The horse must have thrown him. How terrible!'

I was angry and upset that I'd been blamed for Reuben's death when it wasn't my fault. I was suffering too. My knees were burning and I could hardly stand up. It was a horrible walk home and I'll never forget it. Poor Reuben lay in the cart, cold as stone, while I painfully hobbled behind.

Back at the stable, my knees were cleaned and a hot poultice* put on my foot to draw the heat out of it. I was in agony but at least the treatment helped. It also helped when everyone realised that Reuben had been drunk and the accident was his fault and not mine.

The next day, the farrier* came to treat my knees and leg. The pain went on for many days, but once I started to get better I was put out to graze in a small meadow. It was good to have my freedom again although I missed the company of the other horses, especially my dear friend Ginger. So imagine my excitement when one day Ginger was led into the field.

Sadly, she was not there for a holiday. Lord George had ridden her too hard and ruined her health. Poor Ginger! She was never the same again and suffered terribly with her back and breathing.

'Look at us!' she said sadly. 'Two young horses both ruined by our owners. Life is cruel.'

A few days later, life got even worse. Lord W and Mr York came to see me.

'The black horse has to go,' said Lord W. 'I don't want a horse with scarred knees. He looks awful.'

Mr York knew a man who kept a livery stable* in Bath, who said he would buy me.

'Black Auster will be well treated there,' he said.

And so it was! A week later I was on my way to Bath, and it all happened so suddenly that I didn't even have time to say goodbye to my dear friend Ginger!

CHAPTER 10

A London cab horse

My new home was nowhere near as nice as Earlshall. I was kept in a stall with a sloping floor that made my legs ache. I was also tied up and couldn't move around. The new work was dreadful! I was now a job horse and this meant I was hired out to anyone who wanted me.

It was not a happy time in my life. I was used to working for people who knew how to ride and drive a horse correctly. Now most of the people who hired me out neither knew nor cared. My mouth was yanked around and strain put on my back and legs.

I was very unhappy, but I always did my best and one day I was rewarded. A man hired me to take him on a long journey. It was a pleasure to work for this man. He did not jab or pull on my mouth and he talked to me kindly. The man hired me several times after that journey, before buying me for a friend who wanted a good, safe horse.

The friend was a kind man but unfortunately he knew nothing about horses. He ordered the best food for me but didn't think to check up on the groom he was paying to care for me. The groom was a thief and instead of feeding the food to me, he was stealing it for his chickens and rabbits. It was a while before my owner found out and by then I had become ill from lack of good food.

My owner hired a new groom but this man was no good either. He was lazy and vain. Soon my stable was dirty and smelled like a sewer. Then I got an infection in my feet. It was so painful and it made me lame. My owner was very angry that he had been cheated for a second time. He decided not to keep a horse any more, and once my feet were better I was sold once again.

I was taken to a horse fair and it would have been fun had my future not depended on it. There was plenty to see as the fair was packed with every kind of horse from tiny ponies to huge shires.* Some animals were fit and healthy, while others were old or ruined by hard work. It was very noisy and people rushed here and there bargaining for a good deal.

My broken knees put many people off buying me. Those that were interested prodded and poked me and looked at my teeth. Then a small, cheerful man with a soft voice came to see me. I liked him at once. He was not like the other people. He handled me gently and I was very pleased when he bought me.

My new owner called me Jack. He was a cabby called Jerry Barker. He lived in London with his wife Polly, their two children, Dolly and Harry, and a grand old horse called Captain. The Barkers didn't have much money but I was very well cared for. On my first morning in my new home, Polly and Dolly fed me sliced apple and made such a fuss of me that I remembered those happy times when I'd been Black Beauty.

Straight away, I was put to work pulling Jerry's taxi cab. Jerry was a kind driver and he treated me well, but that first week was very hard. I wasn't used to the noise and bustle of the London streets and I felt nervous and anxious. But as I learned to trust Jerry, my job became much easier. I worked hard for him, and the work was hard!

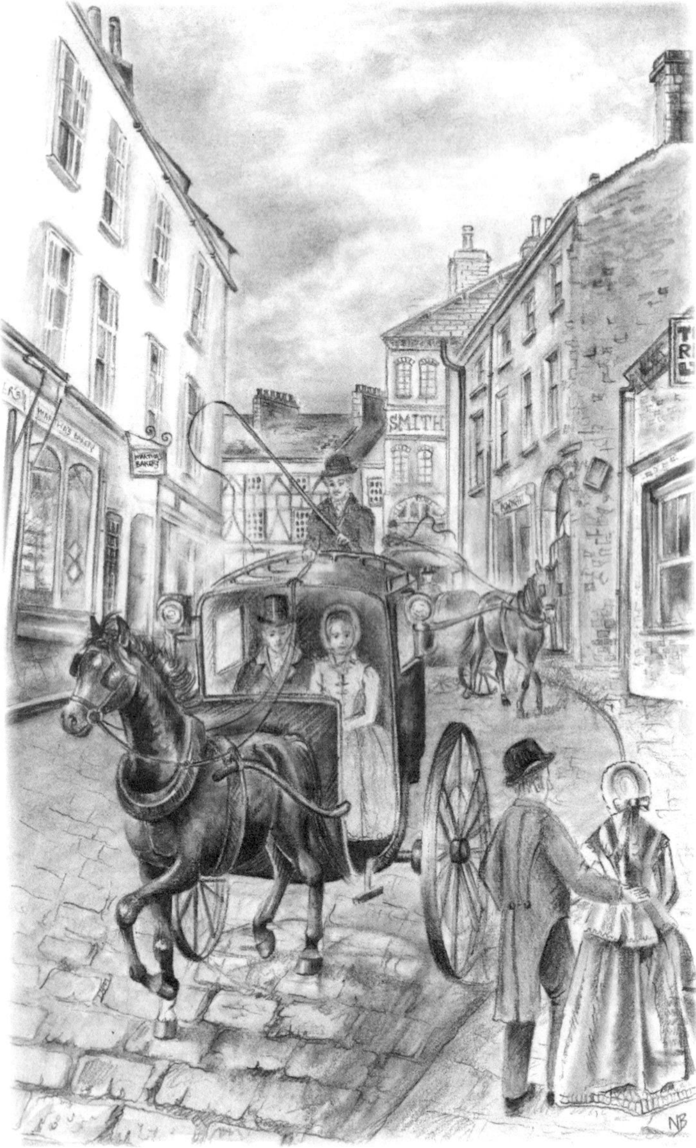
SMITH
NB

Each night Captain and I were stabled in an old-fashioned box with a sloping floor. Jerry never tied us. The stable was clean and the food was good so we were quite comfortable. Best of all though were the Sundays. This was our rest day. Then I did nothing but talk to Captain. He had been a warhorse fighting in the Crimean War* and had shocking tales to tell.

'War sounds awful. Why were the men fighting?' I asked him.

'I am only a horse,' said Captain. 'But I know this. It must have been over something terrible if it was right to kill so many men for it.'

CHAPTER 11

The Sunday cab

I was very happy living and working with Jerry. He was a good man and he reminded me of John Manly at Birtwick Park. Nothing was too much trouble for him. My harness fitted perfectly and Jerry was a kind driver who hardly ever used the whip.

One of Jerry's very good clients was a man called Mr Briggs. Early one morning, Mr Briggs came to see Jerry to ask if he could hire a cab every Sunday morning. He was offering good money but Jerry didn't even think about it.

'I'm sorry, Mr Briggs,' he answered. 'My horses work hard six days a week. Sunday is their day off and they need the rest.'

Mr Briggs offered Jerry a larger sum of money to change his mind. The money would have been useful but still Jerry said no.

'Suit yourself,' said Mr Briggs crossly, storming off.

When Jerry told Polly that he had turned the work down she was pleased. 'Money isn't everything,' she said calmly. 'I would much rather be broke than have you and the horses working seven days a week.'

Money was very tight after that because Mr Briggs stopped using Jerry altogether.

'Don't worry,' said Polly. 'It will all work out in the end.'

And it did. Three weeks later, Polly ran out to meet us as Jerry and I came home from work. 'Guess what?' she said excitedly. 'Mr Briggs sent us a message. He wants you to drive for him tomorrow. He's tried lots of other cabbies but none of them were as good as you.'

Polly was so pleased she was panting, and Jerry laughed. 'You said it would all work out in the end!' he cried. 'And now it has.'

One Sunday, Jerry broke his golden rule not

to work. We had come home late on Saturday night and I was tired and looking forward to my day off.

Then Polly came running into the yard. 'I need a favour,' she told Jerry, as he stood grooming me. 'Poor Dinah Brown's mother is dying. Dinah's desperate to see her but it's a long train journey followed by a walk from the station. You know Dinah's just had a baby and she's not been feeling well. She wants you to take her to visit her mother tomorrow. She'll pay you the money as soon as she can get it. Please, Jerry, please will you help her?'

Jerry tutted. 'It's not the money, Polly,' he said. 'It's the horses. They're tired and so am I!'

'Please!' begged Polly. 'I'd like to think that someone would help me if my mother was dying.'

'All right then,' said Jerry, smiling. 'Tell Dinah I'll do it.'

Jerry borrowed a lighter carriage from a friend, and I was chosen to pull it. I didn't mind. It was a beautiful day and it was lovely to swap the city for the sweet country air.

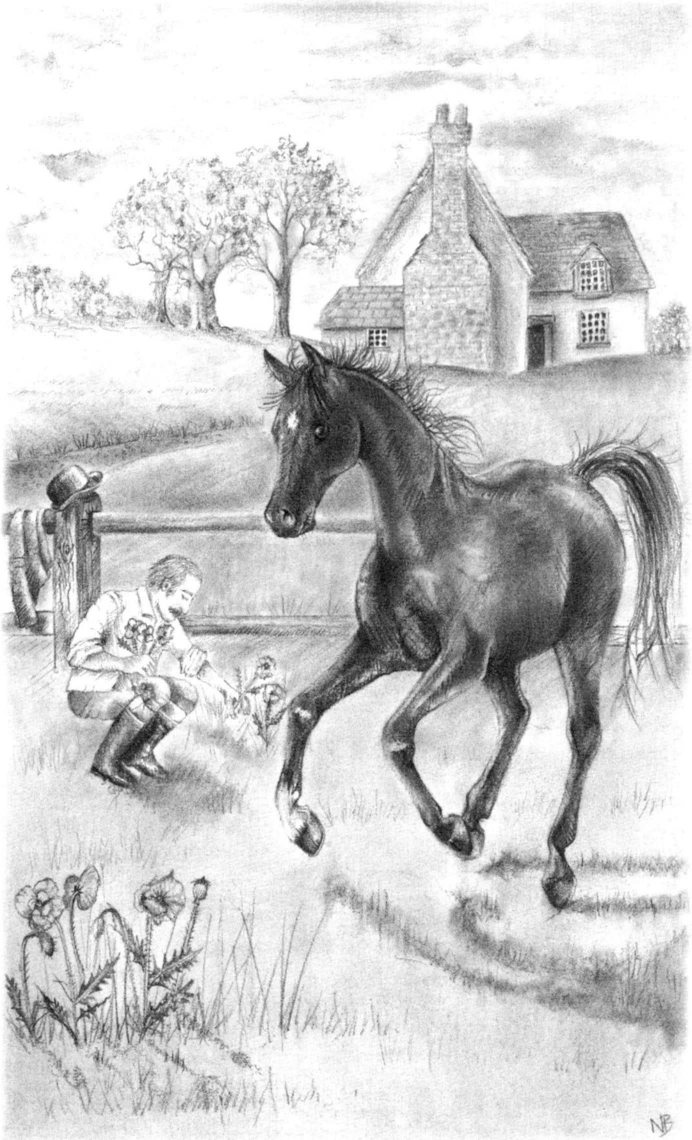

Dinah's family lived in a small farmhouse and offered me a stable in an empty cowshed, but Jerry thought I would like to be outside in their field. It was the first time I'd been loose since I'd left poor Ginger at Earlshall. At first I hardly knew what to do with myself! Should I eat the grass, roll on my back, gallop as fast as I could or lie down and rest? In the end I did everything and it was the best time I'd had in ages.

'Why Jack,' laughed Jerry. 'You're behaving like a young colt!'

Jerry enjoyed himself too, and he picked a bunch of wild flowers to give to his daughter, Dolly. Happily we drove home, and when Dolly saw the flowers she was so pleased she ran around like I had in the meadow!

CHAPTER 12

Poor Ginger

Winter came early and it was bitterly cold with lots of snow and sleet. The streets were slippery and we horses had a hard time. Pulling a cab in the frost or snow is very difficult as there is no grip on the road. We were scared of falling and we also hated standing around in the wet for a fare.

One day I was waiting outside the park when a shabby old cart drove up beside mine. The horse pulling it was an old worn-out chestnut with a badly kept coat, and bones that showed through. I was eating hay, and the wind blew a wisp towards the horse. She reached out her thin neck, ate it hungrily, then looked around for more.

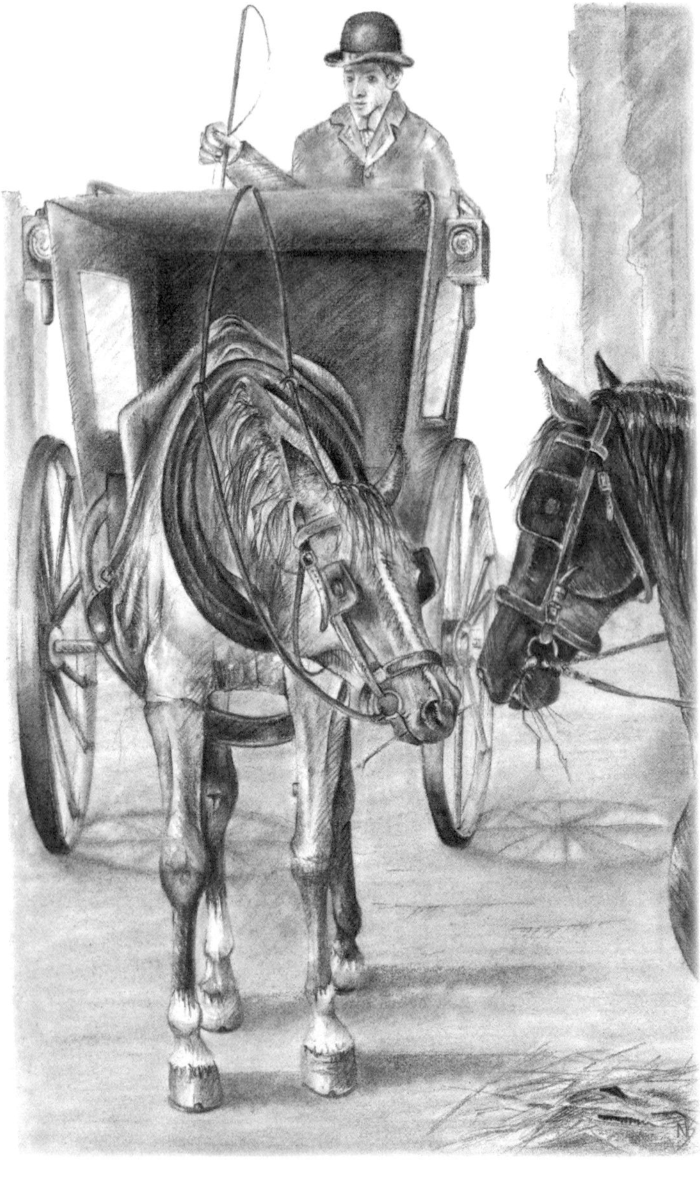

She was a sad sight and I felt sorry for her. She reminded me of someone, and I was wondering who when the horse suddenly cried out, 'Black Beauty? Are you Black Beauty?'

'Ginger!' I gasped.

I couldn't believe my eyes. Surely this thin, worn-out horse was not my beautiful friend, Ginger! Her once arched neck was straight. Her glossy coat had turned lank and dull. Her slender legs were swollen and bruised. Worse still was Ginger's face. Once it had been pretty. Now it was sad and full of pain.

Slowly, between lots of coughing, Ginger told me her sorry story. 'After a year of being left to graze at Earlshall, I was fit enough to be sold. At first I was fine but my new owner galloped me too hard and my old injury came back. I was rested, then sold again.

This happened many times until I was bought by a man who hires out horses and cabs to cab drivers. This man was furious when he found out how unfit I was. He said the only way to make his money back on me was to work me to death. He does too!

Seven days a week I work and my driver whips me badly. I wish I were dead, Black Beauty. How I wish it! I wish to drop down dead and end my pain.'

'Ginger,' I cried, touching her with my nose. 'Please don't say that.'

'Black Beauty,' said Ginger quietly. 'You are my best friend ever.'

Ginger's driver came then. He tugged her roughly on her mouth and drove her away. Heartbroken, I stared after her. Ginger was my best friend too. How I wished I could help her.

Not long after that a cart passed me carrying a dead horse. Its head hung out of the back. Its eyes were sad and sunken. It was so dreadful that I couldn't look. I turned away. But as I did I saw the horse had a streak of white down its forehead. Ginger! Was it her? I hoped it was, for then her troubles would be over.

Poor Ginger. If her owners had been kinder she would never have suffered so badly.

CHAPTER 13

'This cab is taken'

It was election day. The cab drivers were all busy taking men around the city to vote. One politician asked to hire Jerry's cab for a whole day but he said, 'I don't want his posters stuck all over my cab. It'd upset my horses!'

We were waiting for our next ride when a woman carrying a heavy child struggled along. She seemed lost and after a bit asked Jerry, 'Which way is it to St Thomas's hospital?'

It was the lady's first visit to London. She had come up from the country to get help for her sick child. The boy was crying with pain and even though he was four-years-old he couldn't walk.

'The hospital is three miles away,' said Jerry. 'Too far to carry a sick child – especially today when it's so busy!'

'Thank you, but I'll manage,' said the woman.

Jerry would not hear of letting her walk. The woman didn't have any money for a taxi but Jerry said he would drive her for nothing. He was helping her into the cab when two men barged past and climbed in.

'We were here first,' they said. 'Hurry up, driver, and take us where we want to go.'

'This cab is taken,' said Jerry politely.

'Yes, by us,' said one of the men, sitting down. 'And we're staying right here!'

'All right, sir,' said Jerry pleasantly. 'Stay as long as you like.'

He turned his back and refused to move until the men angrily climbed out of the cab and went away.

The young woman was very grateful and could not thank Jerry enough. It was raining when we reached the hospital. Jerry helped her carry her son to the hospital door.

On his way back to me, someone called out, 'Jerry. Jerry Barker!' Another lady, whose name was Mrs Fowler, hurried towards us. 'Jerry, lovely to see you! Especially as I need a ride to Paddington Station.'

Jerry was pleased to see Mrs Fowler too. Years ago, Polly had worked for her and there was lots of news to swap. When we arrived at the station, Mrs Fowler gave Jerry some money to spend on the children.

'You're a good driver, Jerry,' she said. 'If you ever want to move from the city to the country, let me know. I could easily get you a job.'

Jerry thanked her and drove home in a very good mood.

CHAPTER 14

Changes

There had been many changes in my life and more were on the way. The first upset me greatly. My good friend, Captain, was bringing Jerry home from the station when an out-of-control brewer's cart pulled by two shire horses smashed into him. It was terrifying, as Captain was dragged to the ground, then speared by a shaft from the cart.

The drayman,* whose cart it was, was later charged with drunken driving, but that was no use to Captain. His injuries were so bad that he would never work a full day again.

Jerry could not afford to keep a horse that didn't work, but he refused to sell Captain to someone else who might work him to death.

One sad day I was taken to the forge for new shoes. When I returned, my friend's stable was empty. Captain had been shot to save him from further pain.

Shortly after that a new horse arrived. He was a fine looking animal called Hotspur. I missed Captain terribly but I gave Hotspur a warm welcome. At first he wasn't very friendly. He'd come from a very posh home and was pining for his old life. Hotspur soon settled though. What horse wouldn't with an owner as kind as Jerry?

Christmas came and went and we were very busy. The work was hard and we often waited long hours in the cold to carry people home from parties.

On New Year's Eve, Jerry and I took two men to a card party in the West End. We were told to collect them at nine o'clock and although we arrived on time neither of the men were ready to leave. It was a wet and windy night and Jerry had a hard time keeping himself warm.

It was gone one o'clock when the men finally wanted their ride home. By then the weather had got to Jerry's lungs and he was coughing badly. I was suffering too. My legs were numb with cold and it was a horrible journey for both of us. Jerry was an honest man and only charged the men what they owed but they were not pleased.

'What a rip off!' they grumbled.

By the time we got home, Jerry was coughing so badly he could hardly speak. In spite of this, he helped Polly to rub me down and feed me before he went indoors.

It was the last time I ever saw him.

Late the next morning, Harry came to see Hotspur and me. When he was done he left us in our stable as if it were a Sunday. Dolly came to visit us next and she was crying. Jerry, her dad, was very ill and the doctor had been called. Poor Jerry had chronic bronchitis* and the doctor didn't know if he would live. There followed many anxious days before Jerry began to get better.

Hotspur and I were beginning to suffer too.

We were full of energy and bored with standing around in our stables. Luckily a good friend of Jerry's began to use us and he even gave Jerry half of the money he earned. This was a big help to the family.

The next time the doctor came, there was more bad news. The doctor said that Jerry must give up driving a cab or he would die a young man. But what could he do instead? Jerry had to earn a living or his family would end up in a terrible place called the workhouse!*

A week later Dolly came tearing into the stables where Harry was grooming me.

'Guess what?' she cried. 'Mrs Fowler, the lady Mum used to work for, has offered Dad a job as a coachman. We're going to live in the country in a cottage with a garden. And I'm going to school! There's a job for you too. You're going to be a gardener's boy or a groom.'

'Fantastic news!' shouted Harry. 'I'd love to be a groom. When can we move?'

This was very good news for the Barkers and I was pleased for them. But what of me? Jerry was the best owner I'd had since leaving

Birtwick Park. I was no longer as fit as I'd been then. Who would want a horse like me?

Jerry's friend, the one who was filling in for him, bought Hotspur. He also offered to find me a home. Jerry agreed, as long as I only went to a good owner.

Leaving day came too quickly. Jerry was still not allowed to go out in the cold but Polly and the children came to say goodbye.

'Poor old Jack! We wish you could come with us,' they sobbed.

Polly and Dolly kissed me and Harry stroked me gently. Then I was led away to my new place.

CHAPTER 15

Hard times

After a bit I was sold to a corn dealer. Jerry's friend knew him and thought he would treat me well. Unfortunately I hardly saw this man as his foreman was left to care for me. Often I had to carry heavier loads than I should. To my horror I was also driven in a bearing-rein and this put an awful strain on my body.

But worst of all was my stable. It was very dark and the poor light weakened my sight. Imagine how bad it felt being led from the darkness straight out into bright sunlight! It was blinding and often made me stumble. The foreman wasn't happy with me and soon he got my owner to trade me for a younger horse.

I shall never forget my next owner.

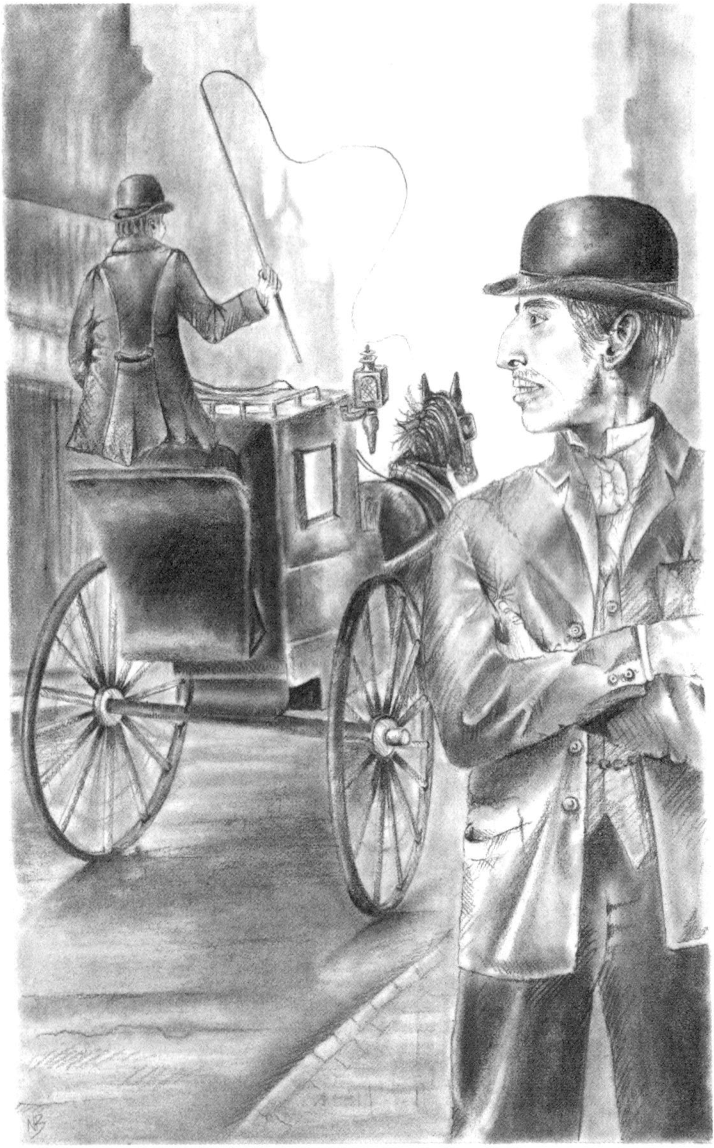

Nicholas Skinner had a large hooked nose, more teeth than a bulldog and a temper as hard as his voice. He was a cruel man and if I thought that I'd been miserable in previous homes, then I'd been mistaken. Life with Nicholas Skinner was the worst it had ever been.

Skinner owned a string of cabs and he worked his horses and drivers seven days a week. Often I had to carry four adult passengers plus their driver on long trips in the hot sun! No one ever thought to get out and walk, even at the steepest of hills. My driver whipped me so cruelly that I bled. Some days I was even too tired to eat my food.

Life became so awful that, like Ginger, I wished I could drop down dead to be out of my misery.

Then I nearly did.

I'd already done a hard day's work when my driver stopped at the station and picked up a family of four. There was a father, a mother, a boy, a small girl and a mountain of luggage.

'Daddy,' said the girl. 'Surely this horse can't carry all of us?'

'Of course he can,' laughed my driver. 'Climb in and I'll show you.'

A porter began to load the luggage onto the cab and the little girl came and stroked my face. 'Daddy,' she said anxiously. 'Please hire a second cab. It's cruel to make this horse work so hard.'

No one listened to her and when the luggage was loaded she was made to climb aboard too. My driver jerked my reins and lashed me with the whip as I slowly moved off. The load was extremely heavy and it was a struggle to pull it, but I did my best until we came to Ludgate Hill. There, the hill beat me.

One minute I was straining with all my might, my driver whipping me harder and harder. The next, my feet seemed to slip away from me and I crashed to the ground, landing on my side.

Badly winded, I lay where I'd fallen and hoped I was dying. Around me people were panicking but over the noise I could hear that sweet little girl's voice.

'Oh!' she kept saying.

'That poor horse, and it's all our fault.'

Finally someone came and unhitched my cab.

A policeman shouted orders but I kept my eyes closed. My breath came in short rasps and a man poured a liquid into my mouth. After a while he tried to help me to stand. I was shocked and badly bruised and it took several attempts before I made it.

Slowly the man led me to a nearby stable. I was given warm gruel and left to rest. The stable was full of fresh straw and it was so comfortable I wanted to stay there forever!

By the evening I was well enough to be led back to Skinner's place where a farrier came to check my health. 'He's overworked,' the farrier said. 'He needs to rest for at least six months.'

'Then he must go for dog meat,' snapped Skinner angrily. 'I'm not feeding a horse to laze around all day.'

'There's a horse sale in ten days. Why not feed him up and sell him there?' suggested the farrier. 'You'll get more money than if you sell him for dog meat.'

'Mmm,' said Skinner unwillingly. 'I suppose I might!'

Skinner was a greedy man and decided that's what he'd do. There followed ten wonderful days of complete rest and delicious food, and I changed my mind about wanting to die. When the day of the horse sale came I felt almost cheerful. Maybe my next home would be better.

CHAPTER 16

Home

It was my second horse sale but this time I was put with the old, broken-down horses. We were a sorry bunch and the buyers who came to visit us weren't much better. They were mainly poor old men looking for a cheap horse to help them earn some money. I waited nervously hoping that my next owner would be a kind one.

After a while, a well-dressed man with a young boy came past, and when they looked at me I pricked up my ears.

'That horse has seen better days,' said the man. 'He's got a lovely head. I expect he used to pull a carriage.'

'Poor thing,' said the boy, coming to stroke my nose.

I nuzzled him gently and the boy laughed.

'Let's buy him, Grandfather. I bet you could make him young again like you did for Ladybird.'

Grandfather laughed too. 'Will, I'm not a magician. Ladybird was a young horse who only needed a rest. I can't make an old horse younger.'

'This horse is special and he's not that old,' said Will.

'The boy's right,' said the groom who'd brought me to the sale. 'This is a fine horse. All he needs is a rest and he'll be as good as new.'

Grandfather looked me over, gently peering inside my mouth and feeling down my legs. He asked the groom to trot me up and down and I arched my thin neck and held my tail high. Grandfather shook his head. 'I must be mad,' he said, getting out his wallet.

'Thank you,' said the groom. 'You won't be disappointed.'

Will skipped excitedly by my side as the groom led me to a stable at an inn next door to the fair. Then, after a good feed and a rest, I was led back to Grandfather's house and put in a meadow.

Will visited every day. He was kind and gentle and he called me his 'Old Crony'.* I loved the time he spent with me. I followed him around the field and we became best friends.

With good food and complete rest I soon grew fit. By spring I was acting like a young horse.

Grandfather tried me in a lightweight carriage and was very pleased with me. Will and Grandfather carried on putting me in a carriage until one summer's day I was ready to be sold.

'I know of a home that would be perfect for this horse,' said Grandfather.

That home belonged to Ellen and Lavinia, two sisters who needed a horse to pull their carriage. They agreed to see me, and Will helped to get me ready.

'Do your best, Old Crony,' he said, as we walked up their drive.

I was nervous, and glad that Will had come with me, especially when the sisters saw me. My scarred knees put them off trying me at first. Will begged them to change their mind and finally they did. The groom was called to take me to a stable, but he was disappointed with me too.

'Old Crony is an excellent horse,' Will told everyone. 'I promise you that you'll love him.'

The next day the groom was brushing my face when he stopped and said thoughtfully, 'How strange! You've got a star just like the one on another horse I knew. His name was Black Beauty. He was a great animal. I wonder what happened to him?'

The groom sighed and continued brushing me until he reached my foot. 'Black Beauty had a white foot and so have you!' cried the groom and suddenly he was examining me all over.

'Black Beauty had a small scar on his neck right here… just like this scar!' The groom's voice rose with excitement. 'It's you! It's Black Beauty. Do you remember me? Little Joe Green who nearly killed you the night you went for the doctor?'

Joyfully, Joe threw his arms around my neck and hugged me.

I didn't recognise this fully grown man with the black beard as the little Joe Green from my past, but I was very glad he had remembered me.

'My poor Black Beauty! You must have been so badly treated. But now you're home! Be good when Ellen and Lavinia try you out. They'll make excellent owners.'

That afternoon, Ellen and Lavinia took me out with their carriage. I did my best and they were very pleased with me. Joe told them how once I'd belonged to Squire Gordon and they were amazed because they knew him too.

'We must write and tell the squire and Mrs Gordon that we have bought their favourite horse,' cried Ellen excitedly.

So I stayed with Joe, working for Ellen and Lavinia, and everyone called me by my old name, Black Beauty. I've been here a whole year now and I'm very happy. Joe is the kindest groom ever and my work is easy and fun. Will comes to visit me and we are special friends. But best of all, Ellen and Lavinia have agreed that I will never be sold again.

At last my troubles are over. I feel I have come home. Sometimes, before I am properly awake, I like to imagine that I am still in the orchard at Birtwick Park. It is peaceful there standing with my old friends under the apple tree.

Anna Sewell
(born 1820, died 1878)

Anna was born in Norfolk, England into a family of Quakers – people who try to live simply, peacefully and with respect for people, animals and the environment. This upbringing was to play a large part in Anna writing *Black Beauty* later on in her life.

Anna grew to know horses well after she had an accident when she was 14. While walking home from school in the rain, she fell and injured both ankles. For the rest of her life she wasn't able to stand or walk for long periods of time, and she often had to use horse-drawn carriages to get around.

Anna had very poor health and never married. It wasn't until she was in her fifties that she dictated *Black Beauty* (her only novel) to her mother. Much of the time she was writing *Black Beauty* Anna was too poorly to leave her bed. She originally planned to write it for adults who worked with horses. She said her aim was to 'induce kindness, sympathy and an understanding treatment of horses'.

Anna died only five months after the novel was published and she probably never dreamed how popular *Black Beauty* would be – to date it is believed to have sold 50 million copies.

Julie Sykes

Julie was born in Kingston upon Thames before moving to Australia with her family. They returned to England when she was five. She was educated in Surrey and studied at Kingston University before training to be a teacher. She taught in schools for seven years before leaving to become a full-time author and mother. She now lives in Hampshire with her husband, three children and a large hairy dog. Julie says, 'I always start my working day by walking my dog. Walking gives me time to daydream and puts me in the mood to write.'

Julie has written over thirty books for children and has won three awards for her book *I Don't Want to go to Bed!*, illustrated by Tim Warnes.

About *Black Beauty*, Julie says, 'I first read the story as a child. It remains one of my favourites so I was very excited about adapting it. It took me a summer to retell *Black Beauty*. Reading *Black Beauty* makes me think it would be much nicer if we could swap all cars for horses. It certainly would cut down on pollution!'

You can find out more about Julie at: www.juliesykes.co.uk.

Notes about this book

Black Beauty is a 'timeless' story because it raises an issue that is still as relevant today as it was when Anna Sewell lived. In Victorian England, horses had to work hard and it was the cruelty to horses that Anna saw that made her put pen to paper.

She understood the reasons why a hard-working man might need to work his horses to the limit, but she didn't agree with the way horses were used to prop up people's greed or vanity. For example, she thought it was cruel and unnecessary to use 'bearing-reins' to hold a horse's head painfully high during fashionable processions.

Anna choosing to tell the story from the point of view of horses makes the reader react strongly to this brutal treatment.

Page 5
***colt** A young male horse.

Page 7
***'It's a hunt'** Hunting was a common countryside sport.

Page 10
***bridle** A piece of equipment, which includes the bit and the reins, placed over a horse's head to allow the rider to control the horse.
***bit** The part of the bridle, usually made of metal, which is placed in the horse's mouth. The reins are attached to the ends of the bit.

Page 11
***harness** The equipment placed on a horse that allows it to pull a carriage or other vehicle.

***ignorant** To be unaware or lack understanding.

Page 12
***Squire** An old-fashioned title given to a man who was the main landowner in a village.

Page 15
***toll gate** Toll roads are roads you have to pay to use. The toll gate is where you pay.

Page 21
***ostlers** People who were responsible for looking after horses, especially at an inn.

Page 23
***hay rack** A rack with bars, usually made of metal, which is attached to the stable wall and filled with hay.

Page 31
***gruel** A thin watery porridge.

Page 32
***inflammation** Swelling.

Page 39
***Lord W** To hide a person's real identity, an author does not give the character's full name.

Page 41
***groom** A person in charge of horses or a stable.

Page 42
***ointment** An oily cream rubbed onto the skin.

Page 43
***Auster** A name possibly meaning 'the south wind'.

Page 50
***dog cart** A cart with two wheels and back to back seats.

Page 52
***poultice** A soft, moist mass of plant material or flour used to relieve pain and kept in place by cloth.
***farrier** A person who shoes horses.

Page 53
***livery stable** A stable in which horses are kept for hire.

Page 56
***shires** Heavy and strong horses that were used to deliver carts of ale.

Page 59
***Crimean War** A war between Russia, on one side, and England, France and the Ottoman Empire (Turkey) on the other, from 1853–1856.

Page 73
***drayman** A driver of a dray, which is a low cart without sides often used to transport ale.

Page 76
***chronic bronchitis** Swelling of the air tubes in the lungs.

Page 77
***workhouse** A place where the very poor would go to live and work.

Page 87
***'Old Crony'** A slang term for an old friend.